The Shelton Brothers
of Illinois

Anne Fafoutakis

Published by

MELROSE
BOOKS

An Imprint of Melrose Press Limited
St Thomas Place, Ely
Cambridgeshire
CB7 4GG, UK
www.melrosebooks.com

FIRST EDITION

Copyright © Anne Fafoutakis 2007

The Author asserts her moral right to
be identified as the author of this work

Cover designed by Nikki Bovis-Coulter

ISBN 978 1 905226 91 7

Typeset in XML by Kerrypress Ltd, Luton
http://www.kerrypress.co.uk

Printed and bound in Great Britain by:
Lightning Source UK Ltd, 6 Precedent Drive,
Rooksley, Milton Keynes, MK13 8PR, UK

1

"Tragedy again has stalked across our smiling fields ... I do not intend to be a master of ceremonies at a show, but a minister of Jesus."

Strange words, indeed, when placed in their rightful context. The funeral service at which they were spoken was attended by over 1,000 people and the casket had cost $3,500 – a goodly sum in the year 1950.

But was it really a tragedy? Had the fields been smiling at any time during the preceding thirty years or so?

The answer surely depends on one's own moral values, for the deceased was none other than Roy Shelton, former convict and the oldest brother of the notorious Shelton gang.

Although he had never been actually identified as a member of the gang, he had nevertheless been tarred with the same brush and was the third of the brothers to be killed in an ambush between 1947–1950.

The Sheltons could be said to have put Peoria not only on the map, but also in the social consciousness of the United States.

Around the time of their notoriety, the population numbered about 105,000. A small town on the Illinois River, Peoria was once known only for its glucose, its agricultural implements, starch, cars and so forth. Quite innocuous products, one might say.

The Sheltons were to change all that. Their terrorist methods and their cunning earned them the title of America's bloodiest gangsters. Their 'reign' was to cover the years 1915–1948 and, although their notoriety was no secret, in the 1950s the surviving members of the family were able to live as wealthy country gentlemen, with interference from no one.

Yet in all those previous years in Illinois, they had held sway over gambling and several other rackets outside Chicago (160 miles away.) They had even honoured Missouri, Kentucky and Indiana with the benefit of their 'experience'.

There was hardly a felony in the book with which they had not been charged at one time or another; hardly any of which they had not been convicted. Perhaps the worst of all their crimes was the ease with which they had corrupted and even bought public officials. Had these people not succumbed, the brothers might not have been able to succeed to the extent that they did. Indeed, reading of their 'exploits', one can only wonder whether any form of law and order existed.

They were formally charged with at least thirty-five felonies. And, coincidentally, they were also responsible for at least thirty-five murders. Among the charges laid at their door? Well, the list is impressive, to put it mildly! Grand and petty larceny, bank and mail robbery, car theft, gambling, burglary, bigamy, kidnapping, violation of the White Slave Traffic Act, vagrancy, riot – the list goes on ad nauseam. Their real forte, however, was the frame-up, the 'fix' and the double-cross.

The leader of the gang was Carl Shelton, born in 1888. Although almost illiterate (he hated school) he was the brains of the outfit and past master at the 'fix'.

Carl possessed great charm and his smiling, unpretentious manner garnered him friends all over Illinois. Many of these friends were ordinary people, but he also took care to cultivate those who could be of some use to him: powerful politicians and well-heeled businessmen.

He yearned to be considered respectable, but he was disappointed to find that living in a fine neighbourhood was not an automatic passkey to the better homes. And although the elite might stoop to buying his bootleg liquor, they would stoop no further. He pretended not to understand this attitude and maintained a belief that bootlegging was in no way dishonourable. He himself neither drank nor smoked and thought anyone who gambled was a fool. But his greatest weakness was women – once there were three of them living in his house at the same time.

Carl loved to talk, to meet people and to spin yarns in his soft-spoken way. He also enjoyed flying planes and driving cars. He owned mostly small cars, except in the mid-1940s, when he graduated to a Cadillac.

He did not go against the law if he could possibly help it. Actually, this was not as difficult as it sounds, since most of the authorities were already in his pay. He tried to avoid a killing, but, once a feud got under way, he would stalk his prey until he had run him to earth and wreaked his revenge. Some people claimed he was humane, generous and loyal, but it is a trifle hard to reconcile these claims to his actions. A very complex man, was Carl.

But perhaps it might be best to start at the beginning.

Ben Shelton, the father of the boys, came originally from Kentucky. There, he had married Agnes Gathier, but without her father's consent. Had Gathier been anything but Indian, he might have let well enough alone. But he was not accustomed to being crossed, particularly by his own daughter. He followed the pair to Illinois, determined to take Agnes back to their tribe. He might even have succeeded, but by the time he actually caught up with them, it was already too late. Ben informed him that Agnes was expecting their

child. Without another word, Gathier turned on his heel
and left, vowing never to see his daughter again.

He was as good as his word, but Agnes was far too
busy to sit around and fret about her father's rejection
of her. In all, she and Ben had ten children, of which
seven survived infancy. In 1885, when she was
twenty-three, Roy was born, followed three years later
by Carl and two years after that by Earl. Agnes must
have asked for a sabbatical from boys, as Bernie didn't
make his debut until 1899, followed by Dalta a year
later. The two girls, Lulu and Hazel, came somewhere
in between – the facts on them remain a little hazy.

Like many others from Kentucky, the Sheltons
decided to settle in Fairfield, Illinois, the seat of Wayne
County, named after 'Mad' Anthony Wayne. (In July,
1779, this General stormed Stony Point, N.Y., in one of
the most brilliantly planned and executed attacks of the
War of Independence. Although dubbed 'Mad'
Anthony, he finished up as General-in-Chief of the
U.S. Army!)

Wayne County is in Little Egypt, as southern Illinois
is called. (There is a Cairo not far away.) The Sheltons
farmed about 120 acres of rather poor native soil near
Merriam, a hamlet about five miles from Fairfield. This
is where most of their children were born.

Ben was a devout Methodist and insisted his
children attend Sunday school – he even persuaded
Carl to play the church organ. He was determined they

should start life with the really important precepts, being a God-fearing man himself.

Carl, Earl and Bernie were not too bright at school. Carl, who was the best of a poor lot, managed to get as far as seventh grade, but such writing as he did in later life shows him to have been almost illiterate.

Partly due to a stammer, Bernie found school a living hell and only got as far as third grade.

More often than not, Carl was late for school and one day the teacher threatened to whip him. The other kids waited to see Carl's reaction. Slowly, very slowly, he rose from his chair and ambled over to where the teacher stood. Then he stretched and drew himself up to his full height. He was big for his age and was actually a good three inches taller than the teacher. The man tried to look away from Carl but, like so many before and after him, he found it hard to escape that steady gaze.

Carl smiled and then, in his soft-spoken way he said, "All right, teacher. Tell you what we'll do. You whip me every mornin' I'm late an' I'll keep score. Then I'll whip you every mornin' when I'm growed."

The teacher could see that righteous indignation would be a wasted effort. Besides, the Sheltons had too many friends in school – big, hulking boys like Cloyd Wilson. He was in no mood to come to grief some night in a dark alley. After that morning, no mention was ever made of either the whipping or the deal.

In 1908, there was a flood which forced Ben Shelton to leave farming and he opened a country store at Thomas Prairie. However, after two years, he went back to farming, having acquired about twenty acres, again near Merriam.

Now the boys were growing up and becoming troublesome, to put it mildly. They started stealing from nearby farms – as one neighbour put it, "They'd steal harness, horse blankets and buggy whips. Steal apples, steal everything they could get their hands on. Everyone was scared of 'em. If they had a grudge against some farmer, they'd stick a knife in his horse or his cow."

The boys started leaving home. Carl married a devout girl but she soon died, though seemingly not under suspicious circumstances. When he was twenty-four, Carl moved to St. Louis, where he became a taxi driver.

Earl's first wife was a girl from a good family but she, too, died early. Earl found the days went by too slowly for his taste and boredom set in. He felt it was time to add a little spice to his life.

Cloyd Wilson, a neighbour of theirs, had a horse and buggy and often gave Earl a lift home. On Saturday, March 20, 1915, Wilson lent Earl $5. They arranged to meet again at 11 p.m. Subsequently, Wilson was to say, "… But then I saw the gun."

He lost the money he had earned that day by selling some shoats – $60 worth. He also lost "a gold watch and a ring". But at least he was still alive and allowed to return home.

The next day, after a Thomas Draper was identified by Cloyd Wilson – and what's more, he had a gun – Earl spoke up for him. He said they had the wrong man. Another neighbour thought they had the right man but that the gun was one he had himself sold Earl the previous night.

Earl and Draper went before a grand jury and were indicted for robbery and conspiracy.

But things didn't end there and it would be hard to say which of the versions was true. According to Wilson, Earl asked him to drop the charges; but even for $500 he said no. Again according to Wilson, strings were pulled to isolate the case from that of Draper. Then Carl returned from St. Louis and added his muscle, to intimidate Wilson. When that didn't work, Carl brought in some useful acquaintances to ambush Wilson. But Wilson also had useful acquaintances in the St. Louis area. A cousin of his, Frank Crews, emerged, to shed a little light on Earl's activities. It appeared that Crews's wife had overheard the Sheltons planning the ambush. Although the two thugs were arrested by the Wayne County sheriff, nothing came of it. Later, Mrs. Crews was threatened, unless she left town. Crews saw to it that the St. Louis police were kept informed and added another tidbit: he knew for a fact that the year before, Carl Shelton and another man had stolen a car in St. Louis.

The St. Louis police went into high gear: they charged Carl with compounding a felony and added a count of grand larceny for the stolen car.

This started the cycle of vengeance which was to characterise the frame-up methods practised by the Sheltons from then on. It also established a pattern which stamped all their activities in the future: that is to say, conflicting versions of what really happened.

While Earl's case dragged on at Fairfield, in St. Louis the Sheltons began their bulldog tactics – they were not about to let go. They found a hobo who would tell the police that Frank Crews had taken a ring of theirs. Offered a horse and cart in return for telling this lie, the hobo was only too happy to oblige. When the police arrived at Crews's house, he mistook them for Shelton 'emissaries' and there was some shooting. One of the detectives lost a finger and Crews was shot through the left lung. When he was arrested, the detectives discovered that the whole thing had been a frame-up. The new owner of the horse and cart admitted what he had done and Crews was cleared.

The Sheltons were unrelenting in their hatred of Cloyd Wilson who was as stubborn as they. Despite receiving threats all summer long, he nevertheless engaged the best lawyer in Fairfield to help the state's attorney.

In St. Louis, the Sheltons got hold of some poison and tried to get rid of Cloyd Wilson's livestock. They even talked their mother into helping them. In a bizarre turn of events, she told the sheriff that Cloyd Wilson's mother had come at her with a butcher's knife! The ploy was not successful.

A friend approached Cloyd Wilson. "Aren't you scared of the Sheltons? Can't you see they're trying to bump you off?"

His response was, "They'll never do it in the open. If they shoot me, it'll be from behind a tree. I went to school with 'em, so I know."

Actually, Wilson's persistence was to pay off. Although the case had cost him over $1,000 (a huge sum in those days), aside from the losses on the farm, he was one of the very few who ever got the better of the Sheltons.

In October, Earl was tried and then sentenced to jail for an indeterminate period. Carl himself spent a year in the workhouse. (He had persuaded the court to reduce his conviction to one of *petty* larceny.)

Earl proved a model prisoner at the penitentiary. He neither drank nor smoked, but he swore a great deal, as did several of the other inmates. After a year and a half there, he was paroled.

When their sentences were over, Carl and Earl embarked on a chequered career. They drove taxis in St. Louis and after a while they were joined there by Bernie, their younger brother. In April, 1917, he was arrested in a stolen car but was not charged. The brothers decided to go to Carterville, a coal-mining town in Williamson County and there Carl worked in the mines. It is not certain whether the others became miners.

Then they 'discovered' East St. Louis, a hotbed of crooked politicians, gamblers and other assorted undesirables.

In 1920 the Sheltons settled, opening a saloon which Carl and Bernie operated. Earl ran liquor in from the south and soon they were befriending the politicians. Art Newman and Charley Birger were gangsters who had already staked their claim there. When they met the Sheltons, they never imagined that pretty soon they would be taking over – like it or not.

Their headquarters was the Arlington Hotel, opposite City Hall! It had an unsavoury reputation, which was strange, considering its location. It was owned by Art Newman and his wife. Like Carl, Art was in his thirties. He maintained that when the Sheltons first arrived, on their uppers, he had helped them out with money so that they could set up their own bootlegging operations. In no time at all, they started strutting around the hotel, making a show of their guns, polishing them and looking down the barrels.

After sentencing Art Newman, years later, a Williamson County judge was to write, "Personally, we think he should be kept in the penitentiary as long as he lives; he should never again be forced upon society ...

We characterise him as a thief, a gambler, a pickpocket, a hijacker, a robber and a murderer without conscience." In all fairness, it should be added that this same judge was not exactly overfond of the Arlington, which he had once described as a place for "gamblers, lewd women and criminals of every kind".

In other words, the Sheltons were in like company. Newman's associate, Charley Birger, was addicted to silk shirts and silk underwear. His parents had left Russia and settled in Harrisburg, Illinois. Charley grew up in the coal-mining community and rumour had it that he had once been in the U.S. Cavalry.

With Prohibition, he became the chief bootlegger in his county. He usually went around with $4,000 or $5,000 in his pockets and had the disquieting habit of standing in the courthouse square in Harrisburg and making sure everyone saw him counting it. If he saw a boy shoeless and in rags, he would buy him clothes and shoes and then send him home. "Tell your mother Charley Birger did this for you." At that time, such a gesture didn't use up more than $8. The boy would be grateful and eventually find himself with others in the same situation, working for Birger. They would be given 50¢ or $1 to steal a car which Birger would use for his bootlegging activities. Once it had outlived its purpose, he would tell the insurance company where it could be found and they would pay him the reward money of up to $50. This was what was laughingly called 'co-operating with the authorities'!

Then, in 1922, Harrisburg got itself a new sheriff, John Small. Birger sent his representative to offer $75,000 as the price for keeping quiet and doing what he was told. Small gave his answer loud and clear.

"You go tell Birger this: if he bootlegs and makes a million dollars, it's all his, but if I catch him, the law'll take its course!"

Small was as good as his word and Birger found himself in prison. When he came out, he said to the sheriff, "I tried to buy you and I couldn't and I didn't have sense enough to get out. But I'm leaving the county now and I won't be back as long as you're sheriff. And I won't let any of my boys kill anybody in your county." Birger had seen at first-hand that Small meant business. So Birger went over to Williamson County, where he opened a roadhouse. Soon, he, the Sheltons and Art Newman became 'partners'.

The Sheltons' roadhouse was near Herrin, which was a coal town, like so many others in the area. All these coal towns had one thing in common: thugs, gamblers and bootleggers. However, if you wanted to wield real power, you let the locals run their business but under *your* aegis. Birger and the Sheltons had the brains – and the guns – to ensure co-operation. The locals would pay for protection and buy their liquor only from the gang.

The authorities turned a blind eye to this monopoly. As a matter of fact it suited them just fine, as the crime could now be pinpointed, where before they had been run off their feet trying to catch up with one outbreak here and another there. It also filled their pockets that much more! Here, the officials were owned by Birger, there by the Sheltons.

It is hard to believe that in the 20s in Williamson County there were ravines in which dwelt barefoot hill people at the same time as new towns were being built. Money was plentiful because the pay was good; industries were springing up all over the place. Loafers and other ne'er-do-wells could find favour and jobs with Birger and the Sheltons.

In the 1870s, Herrin had been the site of feuds and thus 'Bloody Williamson County' was born. In June, 1922, the 'sobriquet' was revived when twenty-two 'scabs' were killed by striking miners. The grand jury found 434 indictments on its plate, but as the jurors would not vote or even decide on a verdict, no one was convicted. There wasn't even a rap on the knuckles for what became known as the Herrin Massacre.

In point of fact, the Sheltons were in no way responsible for this. However, when they saw that no punishment was forthcoming for this crime, they realised that they could carry on with impunity. This led to gang warfare.

But now another ugly monster reared its head. The sinister Ku Klux Klan made its presence felt. In Williamson and Saline Counties alone, the organisation could boast 4,000 adherents. Most of these were people who had seen the total paralysis of law enforcement, were disgusted with the general situation and wanted only to be rid of the gangs and their thugs, who were running people's lives.

The inevitable happened: the Klan and the Sheltons were on a course for collision. When an unsavoury character by the name of S. Glen Young took over the Klan in Herrin County, the fireworks started. He threatened drastic measures and he was as good as his word. At the beginning of January, 1924, thirty-five people were arrested, 'arrested' being a euphemism for what really took place.

Mopping-up operations began in earnest. Within weeks, coroners' inquests were incomplete and verdicts became frighteningly monotonous. 'Death from unknown causes' or 'death by person or persons unknown' were ruled in about 153 cases. All this within a few months in Williamson County alone. The sobriquet was not about to be relinquished.

Having done a good laundry job in Williamson and Herrin, Young next decided that East St. Louis was in urgent need of his services. As he drove there, accompanied by his wife, they were ambushed and shot. Although they survived, the Klan killed a Shelton gunman anyway, for good measure.

It was a tit-for-tat war between the Shelton gang and the Ku Klux Klan and after a few fights – fist and otherwise – the brothers were heard of no more. For a while, that is.

Meanwhile, indictments were being voted by juries, too afraid of the Klan to do otherwise. One man remembered that, "They indicted pret' near everyone made an ugly face at 'em. It was pretty bad around here. They'd get a Ku Klux Klan grand jury and people'd swear to anything. We didn't have no law."

In fact, most of these indictments came to nothing. For at least thirty years they simply gathered dust in the various court houses and for a very good reason: 1924 was an election year and the Klan didn't want to appear too heavy-handed. They reasoned that once they strengthened their grip, politically, things would change. They would not be backward in coming forward.

In September, the jack-in-the-box Sheltons popped up again in a rather picaresque episode. They tried to rob a bank at Kincaid, near Springfield, the capital of Illinois.

Except for the fact that one or two people were injured, the whole affair turned into a Mack Sennett comedy-farce.

Three of the Shelton gang strolled into the bank toting their guns; three others were in a car, where convenient parking had been found. The teller had over $7,000 on the counter, but there was $60,000 in the vault to tempt the bandits, although they had no idea of the exact sum.

It so happened that the President of the bank was there and, being a feisty individual, he started shooting.

The noise activated the burglar alarm and one of the bandits hit him over the head with his gun. Another grabbed a cashier and ordered him to fill a satchel with the money lying on the counter and then he made for the door.

But the crooks had reckoned without the locals! When they heard there was a fracas at the bank, they arrived, brandishing their guns. The bandit carrying the loot was shot in the leg by a grocer. The pain caused him to drop the satchel and within a few seconds, the gang had disappeared, empty-handed, but not before several citizens had recognised their faces. This had proved to be one of the Shelton gang's least successful ventures.

Meanwhile, S. Glen Young strolled into a cigar store in Herrin and came out of it feet first. A deputy sheriff had shot him dead.

Now Birger and the Sheltons could proceed without hindrance. Art Newman joined them, having sold his hotel.

All went well until April 12, 1926, when a meeting was held at Charley Birger's roadhouse. Local elections were scheduled for the following day at Herrin and the plan was simple: see that their people got elected by getting rid of the Klansmen who were sure to be in charge of the polling stations. The riddance was to be of a rather permanent variety.

Consequently, the next day, as a witness later told the coroner's jury, "... I saw a string of cars comin', said, wonder what that means, couldn't be a funeral; passed along, the men driving slow; looking at the first car, I saw a gun sliding out, naturally knew what it meant."

The gangsters numbered around 40 and one of their targets was to be John W. Ford, a constable. They ran him to earth at the Masonic temple, which was serving as a polling station. A witness later testified that the leader of the gang was a Shelton and he had heard him say, "Go get him!"

Notwithstanding the date, luck was with the intended victim that day. He lived to stand up in court and tell the judge what had happened.

"One of them took my gun with thumb and forefinger. I said to him, 'Buddy, that's all I have got; I was sworn in here today as Special Constable to preserve the peace.' And he said, 'Hell you are!' "

Apparently the gunman then backed away a couple of yards and began firing at Ford's face. Then there was an exchange at which a friend of Ford's and the gunman killed each other. After that, all hell broke loose. Carl Shelton was in a big car which was parked at such an angle that it blocked the street. He appeared to be in charge of the whole operation. His brother Bernie was in the car, trigger-happy, shooting here, there and everywhere. Someone later testified that "other fellows seemed to be shooting pretty well at random ... Sheltons seemed to be advising the other fellows or dictating as to how they should do ..."

Another man told the coroner's jury that a local thug "was right in the middle of the bunch ... had one of the largest guns and seemed to be having one of the best times of his life ..."

The streets were overrun by gunmen and they had also taken over most of the buildings.

Someone else stated, "I stood there about twelve minutes, couldn't talk to nobody, account of so much noise from the guns, and then all at once, they seemed to have stopped, about as quick as it started ... All the fellows went direct to automobiles, throwed their guns in, didn't hesitate at all, got right in the cars, I counted eight automobiles." He added a chilling postscript: "I knew the police weren't going to interfere."

Plenty of witnesses were found who could identify the men who had been killed, but identifying the living, i.e. the guilty, was quite another matter.

The gangsters had killed three men but suffered the same number of casualties themselves. But at least the Ku Klux Klan had lost its bite.

Now there was no stopping the Sheltons and Birger and bootlegging went into high gear. But trouble was brewing in the cartel. Soon, men were dying in mysterious ways and quite often were not even identified.

The vendetta had begun and the partnership was slowly but surely going downhill. Earl Shelton maintained that Charley Birger was cooking the books to his advantage; Birger blamed the Sheltons for being high-handed and holding people up – even friends of his. He also claimed that his bootlegging was conducted with the consent of the legal authorities.

Whatever the truth – and at this stage it was rather thin on the ground – the outcome was not entirely unexpected.

Gangsters are rather like lemurs or parrots or the big cats: they will go to inordinate lengths to defend their territory. Many people believed it was this which caused the break-up of the partnership, and really, it all boiled down to counties. Birger had his heart set on Williamson, while the Sheltons preferred Saline. This meant that members of the gang had to make a choice between the devil and the deep blue sea. First, Art Newman defected to Birger, who now owned Shady Rest. This was a roadhouse he had built, complete with a cockpit for rooster fights, which proved very popular. Inside the log cabin he had a craps table, a saloon and a private section where he could stay the night. In an unguarded moment, someone admitted that "he'd take alky (alcohol) and water and colouring matter and put any label you wanted on it: Old Log Cabin, Rock and Rye, Tom and Jerry – anything. $4 a pint. Some said he used a rusty pipe to colour it."

When matters between Birger and the Sheltons became a trifle thorny, Shady Rest was turned into a 'private club'. Birger had his men fire on cars they did not recognise and he fortified a cellar in case of heavy attack. Anyone approaching the property would find himself blinded by floodlights. Birger and his sixteen men were to all intents and purposes living in a fortress.

East St. Louis became the headquarters of the Shelton brothers, so they could be where Carl had a home. Here they kept a low profile until such time as the Birger combine could land themselves in some real trouble. They could then step in and take over.

The idea was not that far-fetched. Birger's gang had now resorted to highway robbery and murder. Carl reasoned that, sooner or later, they would be caught; presumably by officials who were not in their pay.

Now and then, members of either gang would have an unexpected meeting with their Creator, but it was becoming virtually impossible to determine whether they belonged to Birger or to the Sheltons, since there were often last-minute change-overs in loyalty.

All this played havoc with the authorities who had, until recently, protected the Birger-Shelton partnership. Now, they didn't know who was who. So they simply washed their hands of the whole affair.

Perhaps it was this general apathy which encouraged Birger to give out statements to the papers. When asked about Carl Shelton, he declared, "Sure I'd kill him if I see him, just like he'd knock me off if he'd get a chance. But he's afraid of me, the yellow skunk." He added that he had called Carl on the phone and "invited him to come down here and shoot it out. He didn't come. And he's got a ... bunch of professional trigger-pullers and roughnecks. All I got here is a bunch of my friends." (Butter wouldn't melt.)

The response from the Sheltons was published in the same paper. It came from Earl who, even though he was ill, was not about to let matters rest.

"To begin with, let me say this is the first statement of trouble in Williamson County ever made by the Shelton boys, for the Shelton boys do not talk. No, we are not given to boasting of what great warriors we are, like Birger, who is not a warrior but a coward." Earl went on to accuse Birger of the death of one 'Wild Bill' Holland, actually a Shelton gangster, though you wouldn't have guessed it from the way he was lovingly described! "… . A young miner, the main support of his widowed mother and his sister … a dear little mild-mannered chap … this awful crime shocked us all"!!! Then Earl delivered the coup de grace. "If the authorities are interested, they will find that Birger has two hot cars, on one of which there is a reward of $1,000 for its recovery."

This was not playing the game; there is little enough honour among thieves, but rarely would a gangster actively seek police help against another. This does not mean they had integrity – far from it – it simply means that, once this started, it could snowball and eventually an avalanche of finger-pointing would result.

So it proved. Accusations flew thick and fast from both sides and several murders were committed. The frame-ups now became commonplace: the Sheltons said Birger was selling narcotics; Newman and Birger accused the Sheltons of mail robbery. The federal authorities didn't know whom to believe. A man called Harvey Dungy, who transported bootleg liquor for Birger, was brought before him and told to make a false statement about a mail robbery in Collinsville. He was to say he had seen the Sheltons there when it was being carried out. Actually, he was given little choice in the matter: it was either do it or die.

When the Sheltons were charged, things started to pop. Pretty soon, a plane flew over Shady Rest, dropping three do-it-yourself bombs on it. Only one made any contact, but it did not explode. But Birger went out of his mind. He ordered two of his men to eliminate Joe Adams, a friend of the Sheltons weighing in at 300 lbs. At the end of December, Birger was indicted, but the warrant was not served on him, even though it was widely known he had ordered the murder. It seemed no one could touch him. But a few days later, Shady Rest was destroyed by fire. In the ashes lay Charley Birger's fate.

Four bodies were found, among them that of a woman. All had been shot to death. Birger was absent but he was convinced that the guilty party was an acquaintance, a State Highway Patrolman named Lory Price.

A few days after the fire, Charley Birger set off to avenge the Shady Rest. He, Art Newman and five of his henchmen murdered Price and threw his wife's body down a deserted mine shaft. (It took a while for the bodies to be discovered.) Then they went to Quincy, where the Sheltons were being tried for the Collinsville robbery. Joined by Dungy, Newman and Birger's testimony helped to send the Sheltons to Leavenworth Penitentiary for twenty-five years. Once there, Carl issued a statement to the effect that "... we are here and Newman and Birger have had their revenge. There is some consolation that we are leaving more trouble behind than we will find here." There was a deal of bravado in this, for, just before being taken to their cells, they plopped down on a bench and cried.

Meanwhile, Birger was collecting trouble of his own. At Harrisburg the authorities arrested him but, perhaps to no one's surprise, they let him keep his machine gun. And soon he was out – on bond. But in two shakes of a lamb's kidney, he was back in jail once more.

Someone who had seen Adams killed now came forward and, too, the state's attorney found one of the gunmen. This time, the machine gun was not in evidence when Birger was charged with the murder of Adams. And this time, there was no bond.

The scales were weighted against Charley Birger and were getting heavier by the minute. Then suddenly, the skies opened. Ethel Price's body was discovered in the abandoned mine shaft and soon after that, her husband's corpse was found.

Birger, Newman and eight of their gang were charged with the Price murder. In point of fact, Newman and Birger were charged with the Adams killing, since it predated that of the Prices'. Although Newman received a life term, Birger was sentenced to death, as was one of their henchmen – for yet another murder. The other gangsters who had gone on trial with them also went to jail.

Now that everyone was safely tucked away, Harvey Dungy came forward and admitted to the Sheltons' lawyer that he had been forced at gunpoint to perjure himself as regards the mail robbery. He even approached the Post-Dispatch and repeated this to a reporter.

The Sheltons were released. Birger, hearing of Dungy's admission remarked, "He's a no-good bum I never could depend on."

Although Newman tried to convict the Sheltons of a bank robbery in Kincaid – the bank robbery that never was – he was unsuccessful, as false witnesses started coming out of the woodwork and again owned up that they had been threatened. So now, the Sheltons had things all to themselves and they went on to, in their eyes at least, greater glory. They settled in East St. Louis and were now regarded with considerable awe. They were the eternal survivors – the stuff of legend. People spoke of them in hushed tones, using the names Jesse James or Robin Hood or anyone else who took their fancy.

Birger had been executed and his associates were in jail – now there was nothing to stop the brothers and their thugs.

They seized the opportunity and deftly turned it to their advantage, bringing in bootleg liquor from the Bahamas via Florida. Of course, their calling cards said 'Wholesale Liquor Dealers', but they made enormous profits. With the exception of Chicago, they had all of Illinois in their pocket. It was even whispered that they had had dealings with Al Capone. One gathers this did not go beyond the whispering stage.

One untapped source was now available to them: gambling. Here they honed their organising skills until they shone, as it were. East St. Louis was their playground and play in it they did.

No officials had ever interfered with the gamblers and the games had gone on for years. When the Sheltons took over, gambling was syndicated; the protection money poured in. This was because it meant protection not only from thieves but also from the law. To understand the size of the operation, one sheriff was offered $1,000 a *week* if he would let just one craps game run. At that time, this was a great deal of money.

There was one – and only one – thing to be said in the Sheltons' favour: the pay-offs were proportionate to the grosses. So nobody starved except the sucker who gambled and one could say in all fairness that there was one born every minute!

When things went well for the Sheltons, they went very well indeed. Their gross takings in 1930 (a good vintage year) were around $2 million, from slot machines alone. Race-horse handbooks accounted for another $1.5 million and $1 million came in from other types of gambling and so on. Bootlegging aside, they made around $5 million a year.

Of the $2 million from the slot machines, the net profits would actually leave the Sheltons with $840,000 a year. $300,000 went for political protection, $750,000 was paid to those on whose property the slot machines were located, and so forth. Even the $840,000 was whittled down a little more since thugs, collectors and other gunmen required salaries. Nevertheless, it is estimated that between 1928–1932, they netted around $2 million. No one ever estimated their profits in bootlegging. Of course, none of this would have been achieved without clear thinking and strong-arm tactics. The Sheltons got to the top of the mug-shot brigade because they were canny. As the man says, 'You don't need a college education.'

The politicians were in their pay, as were the authorities. The other gangsters held them at arm's length, for there is no doubt they feared 'the boys'.

Although city gangsters had no qualms about killing, they just did it as a means to an end: either their territory had been invaded or they were threatened in some other way.

In the Sheltons' case, the motives were different. Theirs were more like a vendetta – 'a-feudin', a-fussin' and a-fightin' is nearer the mark. It was not always a matter of life or death that set them off. Someone who had known Carl described their methods.

"Carl'd co-operate with the law as far as possible, try to avoid killings, try to be a diplomat. But when he was out to get a guy, he'd get in his car and start out with a shotgun and blow 'im apart." Carl was a great one for appearances: things had to look good. His pearl-handled frontier-model revolver was always with him. He dressed well and, had one not known of his real activities, one could have mistaken him for a respectable businessman.

For far too long, the Sheltons had gone unmolested in East St. Louis, but now the 'Fearless Feds' weighed in. Carl was accused of violating the Prohibition Law and they added to that the charge that he broke the Dyer Act, having hijacked a truck which he thought was carrying liquor. In fact, the load was $25,000 worth of shoes, but that made no difference. When sentencing him to a year in prison (and fining him $500 on top of that) the judge remarked,

"You are a man of intelligence and ability … I am sure that same amount of energy applied to some legitimate pursuit would be more satisfactory to you and I know it would be much less dangerous … the life of a man who constantly violates the law is very uncertain. They are here today and gone tomorrow. Do you think that you will lead a better life?" Of course, Carl was all for that and said so!

The Feds were now hot on the trail of another of the brothers and they caught up with Earl on July 24, 1931.

He and two of his cronies were in a sinking boat off the coast of Georgia. None of the three could swim and when they were rescued by prohibition agents, Earl panicked and did not resist arrest. He was afraid he would drown, but as the boat had run aground in shallow water, he was actually in no danger. He and his thugs were charged with violation of the Prohibition Law. Liquor had been found in the boat – lots of it.

Things were not looking too bright for the brothers Shelton. In the previous year, 1930, had occurred what was called a political 'accident'.

East St. Louis is in St. Clair County. By some marvellous stroke of luck (for St. Clair County, at any rate) the new sheriff was a certain Jerome Munie, who owned a store. There was no love lost between him and the brothers and there were two reasons for this. The first was that Munie was an honest man, a rarity, indeed. The second was that, like many other people, he did not appreciate being the butt of others' jokes.

For example, when Munie asked one of the Shelton henchmen to account for his movements on a certain Sunday morning, he was told, "Sunday school! Where the hell you think I'd be?"

Munie stood up for himself as best he could. After a couple of attempts to bribe him, the Sheltons finally realised that he could not be bought. The next step was to persuade him in very subtle ways to turn a blind eye.

Munie was a Catholic and he was more than a little surprised when Carl and Bernie visited him, wearing scapular medals. But they were knocking on a deaf man's door. Munie didn't think twice about arresting them when he could. Pity about the scapular medals.

Labour racketeering was a source that had yet to be tapped so of course, it was next on the agenda of the various bootleggers.

Oliver Alden Moore, a union leader, supposedly a man to be reckoned with, had refused a bribe from Carl and Bernie. It was a nice, fat one – $30,000 – but he refused to leave. The next natural step was a threat and he still wouldn't leave. So the Sheltons told him, "Well, Moore, we know where you live." Soon after that, Moore was murdered.

The Sheltons were neither charged nor convicted for this killing. Maybe if they had been, local sentiment would not have run so high. A union leader had been shot dead and the labour element in the town – and in East St. Louis it was in the majority – started to seethe. The Sheltons' 'popularity' hit an all-time low. Also, although they maintained they had never been involved in prostitution, their employees, especially the bootleggers, had introduced whores into nice neighbourhoods and they used their leisure time in standing outside honest businesses, making threats. So that was one more strike against the Sheltons.

Despite his 'big guy' image, Bernie had never managed to outgrow the habit of hanging around street corners waiting for the girls to go by, making the inevitable remarks. If their escorts demurred, they would get a haymaker. One time he and a friend took two girls to the best restaurant in the city. They picked a booth which was already occupied by a boy and girl from the local high school. When the boy refused to leave the booth, Bernie began to slug him. But the boy was in luck, sort of. It just so happened that Carl entered the restaurant just then and after one look from those piercing eyes, Bernie left the place. Carl told the boy he was very sorry for what had happened and tried to make amends. Insisting the boy take the money he was being offered, Carl added, "Sit down and enjoy yourself. The Sheltons aren't in town to interfere with decent citizens."

Now the temperature started to rise. In 1932, a new Governor arrived in Illinois, an honest man by the name of Henry Horner. At last, Munie had someone to help him – it was high time. He created the Southern Illinois Crime Commission: six intrepid men who wore a badge and just happened to be good with a gun.

Munie wanted East St. Louis cleaned *up* before it was cleaned *out*. He told his men that the Sheltons' arrest was to be priority number one. That's what he told them – officially. They were canny enough to read between the lines: get the Sheltons out by persuasion or by 'elimination' of a more permanent kind.

When Munie picked Carl up, he told him, "Let's get this thing straight. There's nobody I know of wants you in St. Clair Country."

Carl replied, "I don't know if you know it or not, but I'm your friend."

Munie smiled. "I appreciate that."

At this point, Carl began to see the writing on the wall. "But what am I going to do? How am I going to live?"

Munie looked him in the eye and made a suggestion. "If I were you, I'd take your pistols and guns and go from town to town. 'Here is (sic) the notorious Shelton Boys in person!' You could make a million."

That was enough for Carl and he was out of East St. Louis. He had married a second time and this wife died, too. There was no mystery about this death, either. He returned to Wayne County and ran some farms he owned there.

Meanwhile, Earl got eighteen months in the Atlanta Penitentiary for running liquor.

As for Bernie, he was now married to a girl he had dated years before. She owned some land and on it they built a Dude Ranch which they called Happy Hollow. They lived there until his wife divorced him in 1937.

When Earl was finally released, he moved to the farm in Fairfield and stopped his roamings. He was a married man now.

On the other hand, Carl did not settle down, for he had started another enterprise in the southern part of the state. He became a business partner of the local gangsters. In other words, he got a cut from their games: ten per cent if they borrowed his name and more if he went out of his way to bribe officials, especially in areas which had not allowed gambling until then.

Soon, the gang operated freely through the centre part of the state, from Peoria to Cairo. Kentucky and Indiana also fell prey to their intrigues and machinations.

The main headquarters was Peoria, a wide-open town where gambling was ostensibly illegal. Of course, the hoodlums soon resolved this problem. If you gambled, you paid a tax which found its way to a 'Special Fund' of the city treasury. This came under the title of 'Funny Money', though it is easy to see who had the last laugh. The palms of local officials were not kept dry for long. As for the non-local officials, Carl saw to it that they would harbour no grudge. He would drive almost as far as Springfield, the state capital. Leaving his car on the main route, he would wait. Presently, a state official would turn up for his $2,000.

If you weren't a joiner – and some gamblers hesitated to go with the Sheltons – several things could happen, the most common method being the wrecking of your property.

At one time, Bernie took two friends with him and they played havoc with a saloon. They broke glasses, mirrors, emptied the contents of the till onto the floor, etc. When the law arrived, they turned to the owner.

"You're having too much trouble out here lately. Fights, rough stuff. We can't have it. What you need is a good partner. You ought to take these fellows in with you," pointing to Bernie and his friends. I believe the word is stalemate.

Bernie's farm was near Peoria and was euphemistically called 'Golden Rule Acres'. He was mad about horses and was, in fact, a good rider. He raised palominos and enjoyed attending rodeos, even as far afield as Wyoming. Wildly extravagant, he once paid $2,750 for a saddle. His farm was comfortable and the furniture was a reflection of his own size – very big. Bernie loved what he called 'cabareting'; he once became so mesmerised by one nightclub comedian that he traipsed after him when he appeared in other cities.

With the war, gambling went from strength to strength. The Sheltons were well-prepared and their operations were highly organised. Because he couldn't be everywhere at once, Carl devised a brilliant spy network.

He would somehow always know who was sleeping on the job. Bernie would suddenly get a phone call at the tavern where he was a regular and Carl would tell him to stop fooling around. The call would often be from 200 miles away, but Bernie never did work that one out. He was sure Carl had seen him through the window.

Peoria was one place where none of them was ever arrested, because they made sure to keep one step ahead of the law – by 'helping'. One member of the law remembered that, "They were always running to the cops, the sheriff, the F.B.I., with tips on every little crime, to hang it on people they were sore at and to ingratiate themselves with the authorities." Were they invincible or were they just plain lucky? Well, if the latter *were* the case, Lady Luck was about to stop smiling on the boys.

With a new mayor and a new state's attorney, open gambling was, for the time being at least, at an end. The City Hall neighbourhood, where they had their headquarters, was no longer safe, so they moved to the Parkway Tavern, about halfway between Peoria and Bernie's farm, 'Golden Rule Acres'.

But now a new threat cropped up and it was a big one.

In the 1930s, Al Capone laid the groundwork for the Chicago Syndicate, known to insiders as 'The Outfit'. By the 1950s they had become very influential, as one of their number put it, "What they do, they do at elections. No killin' any more, unless somebody big gets in their way. Like the Sheltons. Today they've got it figured out so they get every penny." He went on to expound on the methods used. "Say you open a saloon ... you buy all your chalk from the guy and you pay 7¢ for a piece of chalk you could buy for 3¢ at the dime store. The same with your glasses, your peanuts, your towels, your toilet paper – everything. Sure it costs you more. But that way you got protection. The coppers don't bother you, the hoods don't bother you. And the Syndicate makes money."

In 1941, the Syndicate thought it had found the perfect organisation to represent it downstate: the Sheltons. They put out feelers, but the boys were not interested.

The Syndicate then went looking for former members of the gang who might have become disenchanted or who bore a grudge of some kind. They found one or two, but they were none too helpful.

A rumour spread to the effect that anyone bringing in Carl or Bernie to Chicago – alive – would get $10,000. The idea was that, once in Chicago, the Sheltons would be persuaded (a delicate way of putting it) to agree. But even with that kind of reward, it wasn't easy. The Sheltons were nowhere to be found. By 1945, the Syndicate was becoming not only frustrated, but impatient. The new message read $10,000 for Carl or Bernie – alive or dead.

Five hoodlums arrived from Chicago to see if they could succeed where all else had failed. Two of them had a sub-machine gun and they concealed themselves in the wooded area near the Parkway Tavern. The other three had arranged a meeting with Carl and Bernie at the tavern itself, ostensibly to come to a decision about a cargo of stolen whisky.

Carl's antennae were not picking up a favourable signal. He smelt a rat and at the last minute he didn't turn up. So the Syndicate went home with its tail between its legs. It takes one to know one!

Two years later, in 1947, Carl told the gang that he would be hanging up his spurs – in other words, he was giving up a life of crime. He could certainly afford to do so; there was no reason to continue living under all kinds of stress and he knew that several of the others had had enough. The next stage would be retirement or betrayal.

Earl had settled down, owned and farmed 900 acres on the Merriam Road where their mother, Agnes, still lived. Their father had died in 1944.

Carl came back to Wayne County, possibly because someone had struck oil. He decided to build a home there and he married a Vaughn girl. The Harris-Vaughn families and the Sheltons had adjacent farms and were also in some way related. But there was ill-feeling between them which was aggravated when Charley Harris finally emerged after ten years in the penitentiary. He had bootlegged with the Sheltons in East St. Louis but presumably because he had just spent all that time in and they almost all that time out, there was animosity a-plenty. Perhaps the clincher came in June 1947, when they had a row about some cattle, resulting in the beating and shooting of one of the Vaughns.

On October 23, at eight in the morning, Carl was blithely driving his World War II jeep on his way to pick up a load of soybeans. His nephew, the twenty-eight-year-old Little Earl, was behind him. With him in the truck was Ray Walker.

Coming to a rise, Carl's jeep went down the hill and was out of sight to the truck for a few moments. As the truck came to the hill, Ray noticed a black car behind some bushes, just past a bridge.

Before Carl's jeep could reach that bridge, shots came from the direction of the car. The jeep swerved and Carl fell out of it and, hit, crawled into a ditch. By this time, the truck had arrived and the two men stopped it and got out. They also hid in the ditch, below where Carl had fallen. They assumed he was taking shelter, so Little Earl called out for his uncle to join them in their ditch. But Lady Luck had had just about enough of Carl Shelton. More shots followed and then they suddenly stopped. The black car had driven off.

When Walker and Little Earl realised what had happened, they drove into town, collected Earl and Bernie and, with the sheriff and a state trooper, returned to the ditch. Carl's body was riddled with bullets from machine gun, rifle and revolver shots. The officers wanted to leave the body where it was until the crime photographer could do his job. But Earl wouldn't hear of it.

"Boys, I hate to see him in that position. Let's lift him up onto the road." When they did this, they saw

Carl had been lying on his beloved pearl-handled revolver. Five bullets were missing: he had gone down, guns blazing.

He had also gone down damning. Before he died, Ray Walker maintained that Carl had muttered, "Well, Charley, it's me, Carl. You know me … Charley, you've killed me, don't shoot no more. You've done and killed me."

The coroner's jury returned a verdict of murder 'by persons unknown'. A fitting postscript visited on a man who had for years been getting away with crimes, thanks to just such verdicts. The usual ambiguity surrounded the case. Little Earl had declared he had seen Charley Harris shooting. Walker had claimed to have seen someone unknown to him, but dressed 'citified', with suit, hat and dress shirt! Then the stories changed until the authorities grew as confused as their two witnesses.

There had never been such a funeral at Fairfield. There were 1,200 mourners; the florists had run out of flowers and been obliged to turn away 100 would-be customers. Carl was buried in the family plot he himself had bought at Maple Hill Cemetery. His headstone was next to that of his father.

Carl Shelton died intestate. He had arranged to discuss the subject of a will on the day he was shot. His wife was named administrator of his estate. He had $60,010 in realties. His personal property amounted to $34,401.70. His current account at the bank stood at

$9.20. In his line of work, Carl did not find it easy to get life insurance. He carried only $1,000.

No one ever found all those millions he had amassed over the years.

Nine months later, another bronze casket was lowered into the ground, next to that of Carl. This time the occupant was Bernie, felled by one shot as he was leaving the casino he owned in Peoria. The Syndicate was suspected. Bernie, too, had managed to condemn from the grave. He left behind a tape-recording of a bribery attempt by the self-named emissary of a public official. However unwittingly, Bernie had for once been smart. Also for once, a Shelton action turned out to have good consequences.

Shortly before his death he had instructed his wife that, should he die in suspicious circumstances, she was to hand over this recording to Ted Link, a reporter with the St. Louis Dispatch. The paper's eventual exposé of bribery and corruption in Illinois resulted in a political upheaval. (In fact, some time later, when Adlai Stevenson was running for Governor of Illinois, he decided to make the bribery and corruption in Peoria an issue in his campaign.) It is, perhaps, unkind to suggest that the resultant 'housecleaning' might not have proved so efficient had the officials' chief employers not been six feet under.

Once Stevenson had become Governor of Illinois, indictments regarding the Sheltons and their associates started flying back and forth like arrows out of

Sherwood Forest. In all the ensuing melée, one matter was never resolved: who killed Bernie Shelton? A local man suggested that "whoever killed him probably figured everyone was in it so deep, nothin'd be done. Which is exactly the way it turned out. Bernie's dead and everything's the same as before. And no one cares."

Bernie left $60,010 – the same amount as Carl – in realties.

Earl was very proud of the farm he owned near Fairfield. He was also very proud of the house, which had been remodelled and he spent most of his time there. The only time he left was to go into town on business and then, in the evening, he would visit the Farmers' Club, a little casino owned by the family. Like many people, he was a creature of habit, with regular hours. At home he did not seem to take any special measures for his safety, except for a rifle by the front door (most farmers followed this precaution, anyway). He said, "I don't want no dealin's with any outsider. I've got enough land here to make a livin'. I just want to let it all die down and stay here and run my farm."

Two weeks after he had said this – on May 24, 1949 – somebody propped a ladder against the back wall of the Farmers' Club and fired three shots through a window. Two of them went wide but the third landed near his heart. He was rushed to a hospital at Evansville, Indiana, where they succeeded in doing such a good job on him that he was soon home. The usual guesses again flew back and forth. Although it seemed clear enough that Earl knew the guilty party, he remained tight-lipped about the identity of the sniper.

The investigation went nowhere with some speed and the only outcome was the closure of the Farmers' Club.

The Evansville hospital had not seen the last of the Sheltons. In September of the same year, Little Earl paid it an unexpected visit. He had received eight bullets, but was able to return home after a few weeks. When asked about his attacker, he replied, "I intend to let the law handle matters."

On June 7, 1950, while ploughing a field, Roy Shelton was killed by a single shot which shattered his spine. He fell from his tractor and into the path of a disc harrow. Frank McKibbin, a hired hand, was also driving a tractor, but jumped down and ran to turn off Roy's machine. Two more shots were fired from the bushes but they missed McKibbin.

Roy's wife, Blanche, was on the stand several hours later. She told the coroner there had been no threats, adding that Roy got on well with his help. She could not imagine who could have killed him. As he had never been identified with the activities of the gang, it was well-nigh impossible to find the perpetrator.

Roy's funeral was lavish and a special detail of state troopers was in attendance. Mourners were led by the two surviving brothers, Big Earl and Dalta, and by

Dalta's two sons, Little Earl and Little Carl. The chapel and Maple Hill Cemetery were patrolled by the state police. They were afraid that enemies of the Sheltons might choose this opportunity to finish off the rest of the clan.

None of the five killings or five shootings involving the Sheltons or other members of their gang was ever solved.

Although Earl had sworn he would never be hounded out of his home, after several serious threats directed at him and the others, he decided it was time for a change.

The whole family settled in Florida and soon after they had left Illinois, a mysterious fire burned down the old Shelton homestead. It seems they had left in the nick of time.

So now everybody was in Jacksonville. Their mother and their sisters were there also and it was here, on April 27, 1957, six years after they had left Illinois, that Agnes Shelton died in her sleep.

To her last breath, she defended her boys, unlike her husband. Once they had become notorious, Ben Shelton seldom spoke of or to them.

On the evening of April 27, she had called in Little Carl, Dalta's thirty-five-year-old son. She had always tried to impress upon him how good his uncles had been, particularly the one after whom he had been named. She would tell him how Carl had been kind to widows, especially on Christmas Eve, when he would sometimes send them a whole truckload of flowers; and if he had heard of people who were ill and very poor, he would often pay their hospital bills.

Feeling she was nearing the end, she asked Little Carl to put on the gramophone record of the ballad that had been written about Carl. Then she said, as so often she had said in the past, "He was a good boy, was my Carl. He never meant no harm. He fell in with crooks and they was smarter than him and put all the blame on him."

Little Carl started the record and then looked across at his grandmother. Her eyes were closed and, with a smile on her face, she was keeping time to the music with her right hand. He tiptoed out of the room, leaving her to sleep – for the last time. Perhaps the final words she ever heard were those which coupled her with her son, whom she had outlived by ten years.

> *'He left his dear old mother in sorrow there alone,*
>
> *Living down near Merriam in her little country home.*
>
> *May the angels hover over her, for she hasn't long to stay,*
>
> *And I hope she meets her darling in a better world some day.'*

Finally, it might be worth mentioning the strange way the amount of 500 recurs in the life – and death – of the Sheltons.

When Cloyd Wilson was being troublesome, Earl offered him $500 to settle their case out of court. In 1930, Carl was fined $500 and a year in jail in connection with the Dyer Act, mentioned previously. The first of the brothers to die, he was buried in a bronze casket costing $2,500. Bernie, the second to go, was laid in one costing $3,000. Roy's casket set the family back $3,500.

Was the $500 difference deliberate or a twist of fate? We may, of course, never know.

LaVergne, TN USA
16 May 2010
182865LV00003B/87/A